GETTING TO KNOW
THE U.S. PRESIDENTS

J O H N F.
KENNEDY

THIRTY-FIFTH PRESIDENT
1961 – 1963

WRITTEN AND ILLUSTRATED BY MIKE VENEZIA

CHILDREN'S PRESS
AN IMPRINT OF SCHOLASTIC INC.
NEW YORK   TORONTO   LONDON   AUCKLAND   SYDNEY
MEXICO CITY   NEW DELHI   HONG KONG
DANBURY, CONNECTICUT

Reading Consultant: Nanci R. Vargus, Ed.D., Assistant Professor, School of Education, University of Indianapolis

Historical Consultant: Marc J. Selverstone, Ph.D., Assistant Professor, Miller Center of Public Affairs, University of Virginia

Photographs © 2007: AP/Wide World Photos: 30, 31; Corbis Images: 5, 22, 24, 27 (Bettmann), 19, 23; Getty Images: 7 (Hulton Archive), 20 (Lisa Larsen/Time Life Pictures); John Fitzgerald Kennedy Library, Boston: 9 (Bradford Bachrach), 6 (?1963 by Bill Mauldin, reprinted courtesy of the William Mauldin Estate), 3 (?Estate of Stanley Tetrick, photographer, LOOK magazine Collection, PX65-105 227), 10, 12, 16, 17, 21, 29, 32.

Colorist for illustrations: Andrew Day

Library of Congress Cataloging-in-Publication Data

Venezia, Mike.
  John F. Kennedy / written and illustrated by Mike Venezia.
    p. cm. — (Getting to know the U.S. Presidents)
  ISBN-13: 978-0-516-22639-2 (lib. bdg.)   978-0-531-17947-5 (pbk.)
  ISBN-10: 0-516-22639-8 (lib. bdg.)   0-531-17947-8 (pbk.)
 1. Kennedy, John F. (John Fitzgerald), 1917-1963—Juvenile literature.
2. Presidents—United States—Biography—Juvenile literature. I.Title.
II. Series.
  E842.Z9V46 2007
  973.922092—dc22
  [B]

2006023367

1 2 3 4 5 6 7 8 9 10 R 17 16 15 14 13 12 11 10 09 08

President John F. Kennedy works at his desk in the Oval Office while his son, John Jr., plays underneath.

John F. Kennedy was the thirty-fifth president of the United States. He was born in Brookline, Massachusetts, on May 29, 1917. At the age of forty-three, John Kennedy was the youngest man ever elected president. People were eager to see how the young, energetic president would lead the country.

John Kennedy never had the chance to find out if many of his best ideas would work or not. On November 22, 1963, while visiting Dallas, Texas, the president was shot and killed by a mysterious assassin. Lee Harvey Oswald shot President Kennedy twice from the window of a warehouse. Oswald was soon caught. Then, just two days later, Lee Harvey Oswald was shot and killed by Jack Ruby, another mysterious character. Ruby was a Dallas nightclub owner. Police and FBI agents weren't able to get much information from either Oswald or Ruby.

This photograph shows Jack Ruby (at right with his back to the camera) lunging at Lee Harvey Oswald. Ruby had snuck into Dallas police headquarters just as Oswald was being transferred to a nearby jail.

To this day, many people believe there was a conspiracy, or a secret group plan, to kill the president. Many others believe Lee Harvey Oswald acted alone.

Bill Mauldin's famous cartoon, which shows the Lincoln Memorial statue weeping, captured the grief people felt after the assassination of John F. Kennedy.

Whether or not people liked John F. Kennedy as president, almost everyone was shocked and saddened on November 22, 1963.

Anyone who was old enough to understand what happened can remember exactly where they were and what they were doing when they heard the news.

John F. Kennedy Jr. salutes his father's casket during the funeral procession.

John F. Kennedy was a rich kid. In fact, his father, Joseph Kennedy, was one of the richest men in the nation. John had one older brother, two younger brothers, and five younger sisters. The Kennedys never knew what it was like to be poor.

Even when the rest of the country was suffering through a very hard time called the Great Depression, the Kennedy children went to the finest private schools in the United States. They spent time learning to sail and play sports at the family's oceanfront estates in Cape Cod, Massachusetts, and Palm Beach, Florida.

The Kennedy family at their home in Hyannisport, Massachusetts, in 1937

John Kennedy was called Jack by his family and friends. Even though Jack had everything he ever needed, his life wasn't easy. First of all, Jack's father was really strict. He expected his children to win at sports and get the highest grades in school. He let his children know he didn't care for losers. One of the hardest things Jack had to do while growing up was compete with his older brother, Joe.

Joseph Kennedy (center) with his two oldest sons, Joe Jr. (left) and Jack (right)

Joe was a great athlete and excellent student. He was also Mr. Kennedy's favorite son. Jack had another problem, too. He was seriously ill much of the time. Jack often had to miss school while he recuperated from things like scarlet fever, whooping cough, stomach and liver problems, and a serious back injury. This made it even harder to keep up with his brother Joe.

John F. Kennedy was just an average student while in grade school. He spent more time goofing around and playing sports than studying. He did much better while in college at Harvard University. During his junior year, Jack traveled to Europe to visit and work for his father. Joseph Kennedy was then the U.S. ambassador to England.

Joe Jr., Kathleen, and Jack Kennedy in London in 1939

During this time, Jack saw that German dictator Adolf Hitler and Italian dictator Benito Mussolini were getting their armies ready to take over Europe. Jack wrote his final college paper about how unprepared England was when it came to protecting itself from war. Jack's paper was so good that it was made into a book called *Why England Slept*. It became a bestseller!

When World War II began, the United States joined in to fight Germany and Italy in Europe, and Japan in the Pacific Ocean. These countries wanted to take over and rule the entire world. John F. Kennedy was ready to help defend his nation. He joined the navy and became the commander of a PT boat. Lieutenant Kennedy's super-fast torpedo boat, *PT-109*, patrolled waters in the South Pacific looking for Japanese navy ships. One foggy night, *PT-109* was rammed by a Japanese destroyer and sank!

Lt. John F. Kennedy (standing at right) with his *PT-109* crew

Miraculously, Lt. Kennedy was able to save most of his crew. He got his men to swim to the nearest island. Jack grabbed one badly injured crew member's life-jacket strap with his teeth and towed him to shore. Jack Kennedy and his men had to hide on the island for a few days because it was controlled by Japanese soldiers.

Jack was finally able to signal for help, and the crew was rescued. The story was reported in newspapers, and Lt. Kennedy became a hero.

Sadly, Jack's brother, Joe, wasn't as lucky. He was killed in action when his bomber plane exploded. After the war ended, John Kennedy was happy to return home, but also terribly sad. He missed his brother very much.

Joe Kennedy Jr. in front of his aircraft

Mr. Kennedy had always hoped his son Joe would go into politics. He dreamed that Joe might even become U.S. president someday. Now Mr. Kennedy turned his dream toward Jack. Jack wasn't thrilled about having a political career, but went along with his father's wishes.

When a position opened up in the U.S. Congress for a Massachusetts representative, Jack ran for the spot. He decided to do his best. Jack surprised himself and the tough, hardworking people of Boston. They liked what the enthusiastic Jack Kennedy had to say. They believed Jack understood their problems, even if he was a rich guy.

John F. Kennedy visits with sailors on their ship in Boston while campaigning for Congress in 1946.

John F. Kennedy won the election to the U.S. House of Representatives at the age of twenty-nine. A few years later, he ran for the U.S. Senate, and won that election, too. During his time as a senator, Jack was one of the most talked-about bachelors in Washington, D.C. He was handsome, rich, and fun to be around. One night at a dinner party, Jack met a beautiful young woman named Jacqueline Bouvier.

John F. Kennedy and Jacqueline Bouvier Kennedy at their wedding in 1953

John and Jackie Kennedy relaxing with their children John Jr. and Caroline

Jack and Jackie began dating. They soon were engaged and got married. Jack and Jackie had three children. Sadly, one of them died in infancy. The Kennedys seemed like a movie-star family. Newspapers and magazines were always doing stories about the Kennedys.

During his second term as a senator, John F. Kennedy decided to run for president. He was nominated at the Democratic National Convention in 1960. Jack ran against Republican candidate Richard Nixon. It was a tough fight. Kennedy's biggest problems were his young age and his religion. Jack Kennedy was a Catholic. Many people were worried he might be controlled by the Catholic Church and the Pope.

Richard Nixon (left) and John F. Kennedy (right) during the last of their four debates in 1960

Jack Kennedy worked hard to convince people his religious beliefs would stay separate from his government duties. To show he had enough experience to run the country, Jack challenged Richard Nixon to a series of debates. They were the first presidential debates ever shown on television. Because Jack looked more relaxed and in control than Nixon, the debates helped him a lot.

President John F. Kennedy giving his inaugural speech on January 20, 1961

The election was really close and John F. Kennedy just barely won. In January 1961, he gave a remarkable inauguration speech. He challenged all American citizens to work with their government to help solve the country's problems.

He then asked the people of the world to work together to protect freedom and liberty. Right away, President Kennedy created the Peace Corps. This organization gathered volunteers to travel to poor countries. Peace Corps workers dug wells, planted crops, and taught people in struggling nations how to help themselves.

A Peace Corps volunteer with children in Togo, Africa, in the early 1960s

Not every nation saw freedom the same way, however. In Cuba in 1959, a rebel leader named Fidel Castro had overthrown the ruling dictator and taken over the government. Cuba is an island only 90 miles (145 kilometers) off the coast of Florida. Fidel Castro and his rebel army also took over U.S. businesses in Cuba and even the property of Cuban citizens.

Fidel Castro didn't allow any criticism of his government, either. He soon announced he was a Communist. President Kennedy was definitely against Communism and the way it controlled people's lives. He approved a plan to help a group of anti-Castro Cubans invade Cuba and get rid of Castro.

Fidel Castro

This invasion at the Bay of Pigs turned out to be a big mistake. Castro's army was well prepared. Tragically, all the freedom fighters were either killed or captured.

President Kennedy took the entire blame for the Bay of Pigs failure. People began to worry that maybe John Kennedy was too young and inexperienced after all. Then an event happened that gave everyone more confidence in their president.

Fidel Castro became friendly with the United States' biggest enemy at the time, the Soviet Union. In October 1962, the United States discovered that the Soviets were installing nuclear missile bases in Cuba. Those missiles were aimed at major cities in the United States!

The United States took surveillance photos that proved there were Soviet missile installations in Cuba.

President Kennedy addresses the nation to discuss the Cuban Missile Crisis on October 22, 1962.

President Kennedy stood up to the Soviet leader, Nikita Khrushchev. He told Khrushchev he would risk going to war to protect the United States. President Kennedy demanded that the missile bases be removed. While the world held its breath, the United States and Soviet Union worked out a compromise. The missiles were removed, and the possibility of a nuclear war ended for the time being.

Dr. Martin Luther King Jr. waves to the crowd after giving his famous "I Have a Dream" speech during the March on Washington, D.C., on August 28, 1963.

John Kennedy wanted to create laws to better protect the rights of African Americans. Even a hundred years after the Civil War ended, people of color were still being treated unfairly in the United States. In May 1963, police in Birmingham, Alabama, attacked civil-rights demonstrators with dogs and pressure hoses. In August, Dr. Martin Luther King Jr. gave a powerful speech calling for people of all races to live together in peace. These events inspired President Kennedy to push a new civil rights bill through Congress. This bill was made into law soon after President Kennedy died.

President Kennedy outside the Oval Office with John Jr., Caroline, and Caroline's pony, Macaroni

No one knows what would have happened if President Kennedy had lived to serve a second term. John Kennedy laid out plans that he was never able to complete. He started a space program that aimed to put a man on the moon. He also sent thousands of troops into South Vietnam to prevent it from being overrun by Communists. Probably the most important thing President Kennedy did was to help individual citizens realize they had the power to make their country, and even the world, a better place.